GHOSTS of the O.K. CORRAL

and Other Hauntings of Tombstone, Arizona

by Matt Chandler

CAPSTONE PRESS
a capstone imprint

Capstone Captivate is published by Capstone Press, an imprint of Capstone.
1710 Roe Crest Drive
North Mankato, Minnesota 56003
www.capstonepub.com

Library of Congress Cataloging-in-Publication Data is available on the Library of Congress website.
ISBN: 978-1-4966-8370-0 (library binding)
ISBN: 978-1-4966-8421-9 (eBook PDF)

Summary: Tombstone, Arizona, is known for its Wild West roots. Did the gunfights, showdowns, and foul play that happened there lead to today's haunted stories? Learn about the O.K. Corral and other paranormal hot spots in this spooky historic town. Between these pages, readers will find just the right amount of scariness for a cold, dark night.

Image Credits
Alamy: agefotostock, bottom 11, FLHC 1C, top 9, gary warnimont, top 17, James Schaedig, top 29, Robert Rosenblum, bottom 28, bottom 29, Wetdryvac, (map) 29; Dreamstime: Philcold, 26;iStockphoto: DanBrandenburg, 21, ehrlif, top 28, EricVega, 25, xavierarnau, right 23; Pixabay: dannysantos, (wood) design element, geralt, (paper) design element; Shutterstock: Akif Oztoprak, 27, breakermaximus, bottom left 6, Dmitrijs Bindemanis, bottom right 15, Eddie J. Rodriquez, bottom 19, ehrlif, top 15, Everett Historical, bottom right 6, bottom 9, Fer Gregory, top 13, FOTOKITA, bottom right 17, Hollygraphic, top 11, Irina Alexandrovna, bottom 13, Jeffrey M. Frank, top Cover, Kuttelvaserova Stuchelova, 24, meunierd, 8, Paul B. Moore, 5, Paul R. Jones, 12, bottom left 15, top 19, reisegraf.ch, bottom Cover, Rose Carson, 20, Sean Pavone, 7, SergioSH, top left 23

Editorial Credits
Editor: Renae Gilles; Designer: Sara Radka; Media Researcher: Morgan Walters; Production Specialist: Katy LaVigne

Quote Sources
p.16, "Exploring Haunted Tombstone Arizona." At Your Leisure, Oct. 24, 2014.

All internet sites appearing in back matter were available and accurate when this book was sent to press.

Printed and bound in the USA.
PA117

TABLE OF CONTENTS

THE WILD & HAUNTED WEST 4

Chapter 1
THE O.K. CORRAL 6

Chapter 2
GHOSTS OF THE GRAVEYARD.........................10

Chapter 3
THEATER OF THE DEAD 14

Chapter 4
THE SPIRITS OF BIG NOSE KATE'S.....................18

Chapter 5
THE GHOSTS OF THE BUFORD HOUSE 22

HAUNTED PLACES OF TOMBSTONE 28
GLOSSARY 30
READ MORE 31
INTERNET SITES 31
INDEX 32

Words in **bold** are in the glossary.

THE WILD & HAUNTED WEST

In the late 1880s, Tombstone, Arizona, was a booming silver-mining town. People came from all over the country. They hoped to get rich. As the miners came, so did the outlaws. Those people were looking to rob and steal. Gunfights were common. Criminals were often put to death in public. It was one town that led people to call the western U.S. the Wild West.

Has all of that death left the old **boomtown** haunted? People say the **spirits** of the dead wander the streets. They float through graveyards. They are unwelcome guests at hotels. Others say ghosts aren't real. They say some stories are just people's imaginations running wild. They say there are other explanations for spooky happenings. Read on and decide for yourself if Tombstone is haunted.

Some Arizona towns that were busy in the Wild West have been rebuilt as tourist towns. People who visit can learn about the Wild West.

CHAPTER 1

THE O.K. CORRAL

The Wild West was known for gunfights. The most **infamous** gunfight happened near the O.K. Corral in Tombstone. Virgil Earp led a group of lawmen that included Doc Holliday and Wyatt Earp. They fought a band of outlaws known as the Cowboys on October 26, 1881.

It lasted only 30 seconds. Three outlaws were shot and killed. They were Billy Clanton, Tom McLaury, and Frank McLaury. Some say their ghosts live on in Tombstone.

Wyatt Earp

Visitors to Tombstone can go to the site of the gunfight at the O.K. Corral.

Visitors to the O.K. Corral have reported seeing ghosts. They have seen faded visions of men dressed as cowboys with their guns drawn. Ghost hunters say these are the dead outlaws. They are looking to continue the battle. There have also been many reports of cold spots in and around the O.K. Corral. **Paranormal** researchers say these can be a sign that a spirit is present.

The shootout with the Earps wasn't the only gunfight near the O.K. Corral. A man named "Justice Jim" Burnett also died there. He was fighting with a neighbor over land. The man gunned Burnett down in 1897. More than 100 years later, there have been ghost sightings. They are of an old man. He is seen wandering near the spot where Burnett was killed. Whenever a person comes up to him, he disappears. Could it be Burnett back for revenge?

Ghosts of dead men may not be all that haunts the O.K. Corral. People have reported hearing the mysterious sounds of horses stomping around inside the corral as well. But no horses are nearby.

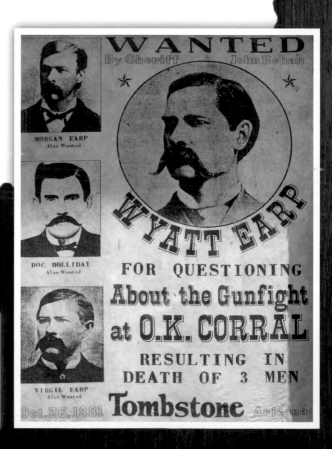

WANTED
By Sheriff John Behan

MORGAN EARP
Also Wanted

DOC HOLLIDAY
Also Wanted

VIRGIL EARP
Also Wanted

WYATT EARP
FOR QUESTIONING
About the Gunfight
at O.K. CORRAL
RESULTING IN
DEATH OF 3 MEN
Oct. 26, 1881 Tombstone Arizona

Even though they were lawmen, the Earps and Holliday were wanted by the law in connection with the gunfight.

Name: Virgil Earp
Job: city marshal of Tombstone
Cause of Death: illness, 1905
Ghost Sightings: said to appear in the street near where he was shot during the gunfight

Name: Frank McLaury
Job: rancher
Cause of Death: shot by Virgil Earp during the gunfight, 1881
Ghost Sightings: seen many times with his gun drawn near the O.K. Corral

Name: Doc Holliday
Job: dentist
Cause of Death: illness, 1887
Ghost Sightings: spotted hanging around Big Nose Kate's Saloon

Name: Billy Clanton
Job: ranch hand
Cause of Death: shot by Virgil and Morgan Earp during the gunfight, 1881
Ghost Sightings: regularly seen near his grave in the Boothill Cemetery

CHAPTER 2
GHOSTS OF THE GRAVEYARD

One of the most common places people report seeing ghosts is in graveyards. It is said that the spirits of the dead can rise from their graves. Boothill Graveyard in Tombstone is home to more than 200 bodies. Most are men. Many had violent deaths. Sightings of ghosts have been reported for decades. This includes ghosts of the men killed in the O.K. Corral shootout. Glowing **orbs** of light have also been seen. They come out of the darkness. Are they the spirits of the dead?

The most famous ghost of the graveyard is Billy Clanton. He was one of the men killed at the O.K. Corral. Visitors claim to have seen him walking toward town. Tourists often take photos of Clanton's grave. In some cases, visitors have discovered something spooky. In the background of the photos appears a fuzzy image. It looks like a person standing next to Clanton's grave marker. The tourists know there was no one there when they took the photo. So who, or what, is it? It is one of the ghostly mysteries of the Boothill Graveyard.

Some people say orbs are spirits of the dead. People have reported seeing them at graveyards throughout the world.

Billy Clanton's tombstone

BILLY
CLANTON
KILLED
OCT. 26, 1881

In the 1930s, Boothill Graveyard became a popular tourist spot. With the tourists came thieves. Headstones were stolen. Even bodies were taken from their resting places. Ghost hunters say disturbing graves is a bad idea. It can anger the spirits of the dead.

Today, Boothill Cemetery has been **restored**. It is once again popular with tourists. It even has a large gift shop. The shop is at the entrance to the cemetery. People are still reporting hauntings at the cemetery. Visitors claim to see misty figures. They float through the cemetery.

A manager at the Boothill Gift Shop said she believes the ghosts of Boothill haunt the store. The ghosts move things around the shop. People say they even steal money from the cash register.

tombstone in Boothill Cemetery

FREAKY FACT

A woman known as
China Mary is buried
in Boothill. The
ghost of a woman in
a red dress is often
reported floating near
Mary's grave.

CHAPTER 3

THEATER OF THE DEAD

The Bird Cage Theatre might be the most haunted place in Tombstone. More than 30 different ghosts are said to haunt the old saloon. The earliest reports came in 1921. A new high school was built. It was across the street from the theater. Students walking by heard laughter and music. It was coming from inside the building. That was impossible. It had been abandoned for years. Soon, reports of paranormal activity increased. Students stopped walking past the Bird Cage.

In the 1980s, a man named William Hunley owned the Bird Cage. He said he had a terrifying encounter one evening. Hunley was in the theater. He was holding a **séance**. An invisible being began choking him. He gasped for air and turned red as the ghost gripped his neck. Suddenly, the spirit let go. Witnesses **verified** this account. Hunley was shaken from the event. He also had bruises on his neck for weeks after the attack.

The Bird Cage Theatre opened on Christmas Eve in 1881.

The Bird Cage Theatre is one of the only places in Tombstone where a violent ghost has been reported.

The haunting of the Bird Cage continues to this day. It is now a tourist attraction. A worker said she started to leave a recorder out at night. She wanted to record any sounds after closing. One day, she came in and listened to the tape. She heard a terrifying recording of what might be ghosts. A woman screamed. She said, "Let me out!" Her voice was followed by the sound of a man. He yelled, "Sit back down!" Still, the employees of the Bird Cage aren't afraid. They love to share ghostly tales of the dead.

More than 100 bullet holes are still in the building of the Bird Cage Theatre.

FIRE GHOSTS

In the 1880s, Tombstone was hit by two major fires. More than 40 people died in the blazes. Today, there are reports of ghostly figures. They wander the streets. Their faces are badly burned. People also smell smoke where there is no fire.

CHAPTER 4

THE SPIRITS OF BIG NOSE KATE'S

Big Nose Kate's Saloon is a popular tourist attraction in Tombstone. It was built on land that once housed the Grand Hotel. The hotel burned to the ground in 1882. The new building was built over the hotel's basement. More than 100 years later, the basement at Big Nose Kate's is said to be one of the most haunted places in Tombstone.

Reports of ghosts in the basement began when the space was being rebuilt. In the darkness, workers heard a scraping noise. They shined their flashlights. But they saw nothing. They guessed it was a rat or other animal. Then they heard a low moaning. It was coming from the same area of the dark basement. Was it a ghost? The men didn't wait around to find out. They quickly left.

Visitors can get food and beverages at Big Nose Kate's, just like Wyatt Earp and Doc Holliday did in the past.

Big Nose Kate's pays tribute to the history of Tombstone in many ways. One is by having two **mannequins**. They are dressed as residents of Tombstone from the 1880s. The mannequins are fun for visitors to look at . . . until they come to life!

One night in 1998, a man was in the saloon. He was interviewing for a job. As he talked with the manager, both men noticed movement. It was coming from the balcony. One of the mannequins was dressed as a woman. It began to move forward. The men froze. The mannequin continued to move toward the balcony railing. Suddenly, it flipped over and crashed to the floor below. As they watched, the male mannequin turned its head. It looked at where the other mannequin once stood. The men leaped from their chairs and ran from the building.

Mannequins, dolls, chairs, clocks, and music boxes have all been reportedly haunted by ghosts.

THE SWAMPER'S TREASURE

The Grand Hotel where Big Nose Kate's Saloon stands today was once home to a handyman. He was nicknamed "the Swamper." Legend says the Swamper tunneled through the basement to a mine shaft. There, he stashed a fortune of silver. After the hotel burned down, his ghost was seen wandering around the property. Some people think he has returned from the dead to guard his treasure.

CHAPTER 5

THE GHOSTS OF THE BUFORD HOUSE

The ghost of George Daves is legendary in Tombstone. In 1888, Daves was 21 years old. He was living in what today is known as the Buford House. He was planning to marry his girlfriend, but suddenly she left him. Daves was heartbroken. He died soon after. For more than 100 years, people have reported seeing his ghost. He wanders through the house and yard. Witnesses say he looks sad. Could he be waiting for his love to return?

The Buford House was a bed and breakfast in the early 2000s. In 2002, the owners brought in a team of ghost hunters to investigate strange reports. While the crew was setting up, a mysterious light appeared. They walked toward it. The light moved across the wall and disappeared. There was no explanation of where it could have come from.

Crew members took many photos. Upon review, they found one terrifying image. A shadowy cowboy was reflected in a mirror. Could it have been one of Tombstone's dead returning for a visit?

Many people tell stories of ghosts being seen in mirrors.

Daves wasn't the only person to meet his end at the Buford House. In the 1880s, three of the Buford children got sick. They died in the home. Ghost hunters say child ghosts often play tricks. Visitors to the Buford House have said the lights turn on and off on their own. Objects are moved. Later, they are found hidden in other parts of the house. Are the Buford children having the fun in death that they missed out on in life?

Today, the house is a private home. The owners say they haven't seen any ghosts yet. But they have heard mysterious voices and felt an eerie presence of something unexplained.

Are Tombstone's ghosts and other eerie happenings real? Or are they just **folklore** and imagination? There may never be proof that ghosts are real. People may never know for sure if the ghost tales about Tombstone are true. Just in case, if you ever make it to Tombstone, keep an eye out for them!

The piano in one Tombstone bar is said to suddenly play when no one is there. It plays a song called "Red River Valley," which was popular in the 1800s.

FREAKY FACT

At the height of the silver boom, there were more than 100 saloons in Tombstone. Today, the ghosts of cowboys are often reported sitting in the bars.

Haunted Places of
TOMBSTONE

1. **The Bird Cage Theatre**

2. **Boothill Cemetery**

3. **Big Nose Kate's Saloon**

4. **The Buford House**

5. **O.K. Corral**

MORE HAUNTED PLACES IN TOMBSTONE

6. **Nellie Cashman's House**
   This restaurant might be haunted by the ghost of its former owner, Nellie Cashman.

7. **Red Buffalo Trading Company**
   Wyatt Earp's brother, Morgan Earp, met his end here. It is reportedly haunted by his ghost.

8. **Schieffelin Hall**
   This theater was built in 1881. Unexplained orbs, strange noises, and voices are still reported today.

Boothill Cemetery

Schieffelin Hall

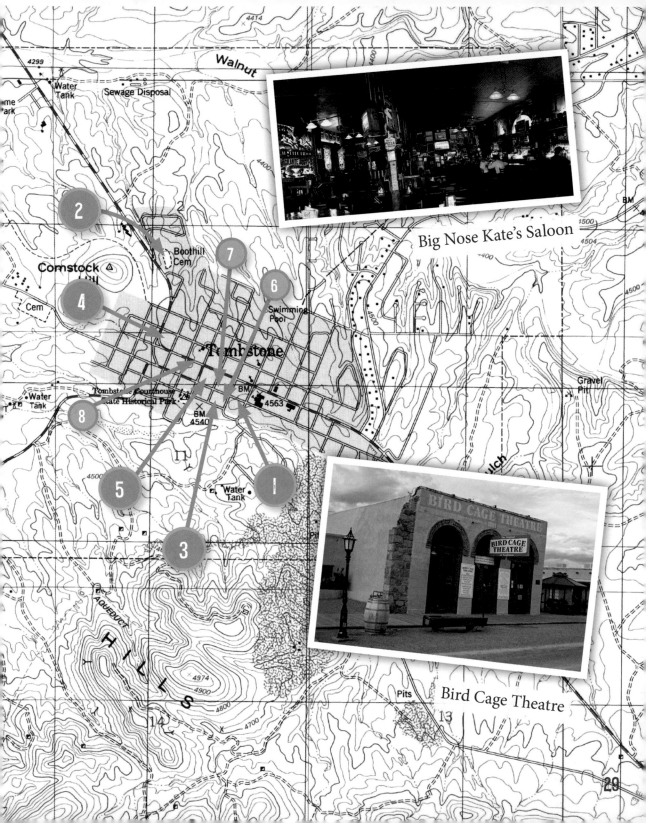

Big Nose Kate's Saloon

Bird Cage Theatre

GLOSSARY

boomtown (BOOM-town)—a community that has a sudden and rapid increase in growth

folklore (FOK-lor)—stories, sayings, and customs among a group of people; folklore stories may not be true

infamous (IN-fuh-muss)—known for a negative act or occurrence

mannequin (MAN-i-kin)—a life-sized dummy used to display clothes

orb (AWRB)—a glowing ball of light that sometimes appears in photographs taken at reportedly haunted locations

paranormal (pair-uh-NOR-muhl)—having to do with an unexplained event that has no scientific explanation

restore (ress-TORE)—to bring something back to its former condition

séance (SAY-ahnss)—a meeting at which people try to make contact with the dead

spirit (SPIHR-it)—the soul or invisible part of a person that is believed to control thoughts and feelings; some people believe the spirit leaves the body after death

verify (VAIR-ih-fye)—to make sure that something is true

READ MORE

Canasi, Brittany. *The Wild West.* Vero Beach, FL: Rourke Educational Media, 2019.

Chandler, Matt. *Famous Ghost Stories of North America.* North Mankato, MN: Capstone Press, 2019.

Cooley Peterson, Megan. *The Bell Witch: An American Ghost Story.* North Mankato, MN: Capstone Press, 2020.

Wood, Alix. *Haunted Houses.* New York City: Gareth Stevens Publishing, 2017.

INTERNET SITES

Ghosts of Tombstone
https://www.legendsofamerica.com/az-tombstoneghosts

The Gunfight at the O.K. Corral
http://socialstudiesforkids.com/articles/ushistory/gunfightatokcorral1.htm

Wild West
http://www.american-historama.org/1881-1913-maturation-era/wild-west.htm

INDEX

Big Nose Kate's Saloon, 9, 18–21

Bird Cage Theatre, 14–17

Boothill Graveyard, 9, 10–13

Buford House, 22–25

Burnett, "Justice Jim", 8

Clanton, Billy, 6, 9–10

cold spots, 7

Daves, George, 22, 24

Earp, Virgil, 6, 8, 9

Earp, Wyatt, 6, 8

Holliday, Doc, 6, 9

lights, 10, 22, 24

McLaury, Frank, 6, 9

McLaury, Tom, 6

O.K. Corral, 6–10

paranormal researchers, 7

photos, 10, 22

séances, 14

sounds, 8, 14, 16, 18, 24